small ones,

swimming ones,

flying ones,

colourful ones and not-so-colourful ones.

Some are so tiny you can't see them.

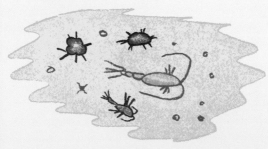

But the little ones matter just as much as the big ones.

And we don't just have animals, there are plants too. Millions and millions of plants: flowers, ferns, trees, grasses, seagrasses, broccoli, bananas…

Our planet is teeming with life.

It's quite a thought, isn't it?

Yes!

A WORLD FULL OF WILDLIFE

by Neal Layton

wren
&rook

Do you like animals?

I love them!

Me too!

I'm sure you'll have some favourite ones, because we are lucky enough to have many different creatures living here on Earth.

Big ones,

Seaweed is actually an algae.

Seagrass is a plant.

So how come all this wonderful stuff is living around us?

Well, all life needs roughly the same things to survive:
  Air to breathe,
    water to drink,
      food to eat
        and somewhere to live happily.

Scientists call this place a habitat.

There are many different habitats on Earth

polar regions

oceans

deserts

grasslands

ungles and rivers, to mention a few.

Because our planet has all sorts of habitats, it is full of all sorts of animals and plants. Creatures look different and eat different foods depending on where they live.

Wow!

Yes, WOW!

Scientists have a special name for this variety of life. They call it

biodiversity.

Oof, that's a big word.

Yes, but it's an important one. If you
look at any animal or plant, its
life will connect with others,
sometimes in one way,
sometimes in lots of ways.

Gosh! How does it do that?

Let's look at one of your favourite animals, the leopard.

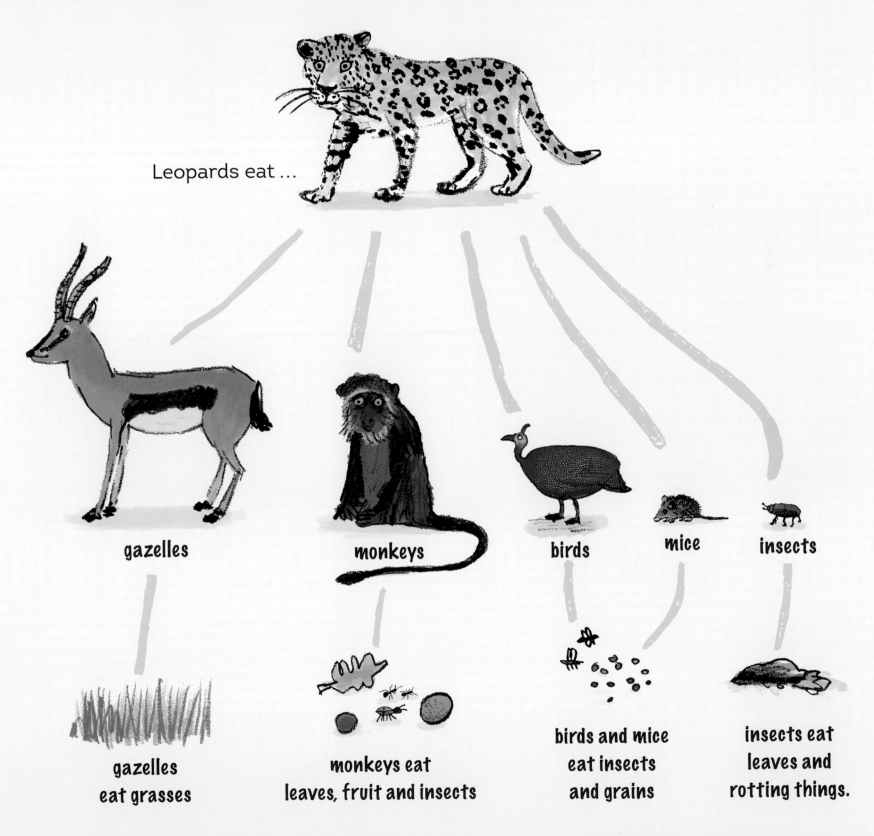

Leopards eat ...

gazelles

monkeys

birds

mice

insects

gazelles
eat grasses

monkeys eat
leaves, fruit and insects

birds and mice
eat insects
and grains

insects eat
leaves and
rotting things.

Scientists call these connections THE WEB OF LIFE because it's like an invisible spider's web linking ALL LIVING THINGS together.

And we humans are woven into this wonderful web of life too.

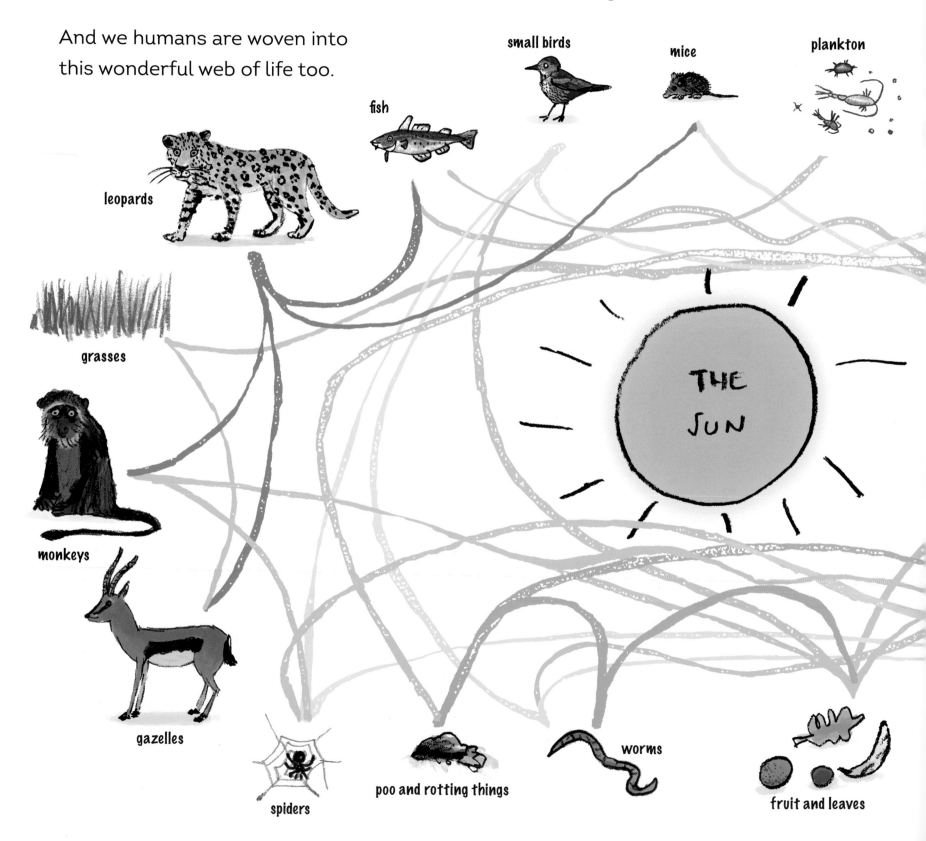

small birds

mice

plankton

fish

leopards

grasses

THE SUN

monkeys

gazelles

spiders

poo and rotting things

worms

fruit and leaves

flies

grains

chickens

nutrients
in soil

humans

beetles

frogs

Do you remember when I said that all creatures need roughly the same things to stay alive?

Well, the oxygen that people breathe comes from plants in the sea and trees on land.

The water that people drink comes from rain that collects into rivers and lakes.

And the food that people eat comes from plants.

We put seeds into the ground and they GROW! Into fruit, seeds, nuts, leaves and grains. Sometimes we eat the plants straight away, and sometimes we feed them to animals that we eat as meat or fish.

The different connections in this web of life can be quite unexpected.

Did you know that animal poo is part of the web too?

And don't forget about the little animals. Bees BUZZ around flowers because they love the flowers' nectar, which they use to make honey. Flowers also have stuff called pollen. When bees visit flowers to collect nectar, pollen gets stuck to them and ends up being carried from flower to flower.

Some animals' poo contains nutrients that are good for plants.

Dung beetles clean away poo and help maintain healthy soil. They also provide food for birds and bats.

This is pollination and it's super-important. Without it, flowering plants can't make seeds – and without seeds, new plants won't grow.

Even creatures that are SO SMALL YOU CAN'T SEE THEM are part of the web of life. Many of these micro-organisms help keep the soil healthy so plants can grow.

Other insects like moths and butterflies can move pollen about too.

There are more micro-bugs in one teaspoon of soil than people living on the planet!

SEEDS

Biodiversity is everywhere. There's a whole web of life outside your front door, even if you live in a city.

Have you ever heard birds singing where you live? There are many different types of birds, each with a different song. Some live in trees, some live in hedgerows and some even live in the roofs of houses.

Mini beasts are all over the place too, from earthworms helping to keep our soil healthy to woodlice and beetles helping leaves and natural things to rot down.

Even plants that we call weeds are part of the web of life. Dandelions are full of pollen and nectar in early spring when not many other flowers are blooming. Their nectar, seeds and leaves feed almost one hundred species of insects and over thirty species of birds and other animals.

Some animals shape the things around them to better suit their needs, and this often helps the web of life to run more smoothly.

Beavers make dams in streams, creating ponds to build homes on. By stopping the flow of water, beavers form wetland habitats for other animals too.

Termites build mounds and live in nests beneath them. Their construction work improves the soil nearby, which means more plants can grow.

Humans shape their habitat too.

But this doesn't usually help other creatures to make homes.

Humans do other things too...

When they plough their enormous fields, they use fertilisers, herbicides and pesticides.

When they fish, they use huge machines that help them catch more fish than they can eat.

Their factories and machines make the air, the rivers, the land and the sea dirty. This is called pollution.

All this is making the web of life get weaker – sometimes so weak that animals and plants are **disappearing.**

And if one plant disappears, so might the animals that use that plant for habitat or food, breaking connections in the web of life.

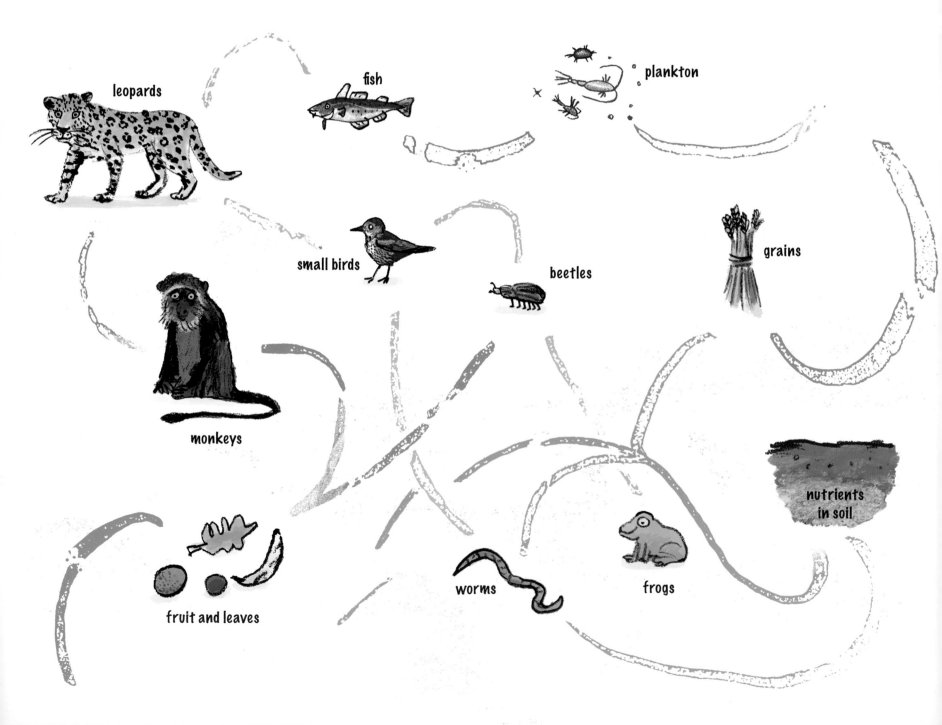

leopards

fish

plankton

small birds

beetles

grains

monkeys

nutrients in soil

fruit and leaves

worms

frogs

Some scientists estimate we are losing more than 27,000 species a year.
And they'll never come back.

HAWKSBILL TURTLE
Critically endangered

GREEN FLECKED
SALAMANDER
Critically endangered

COLLINS
POISON FROG
Critically endangered

DODO
Extinct

ILLIDGE'S ANT BLUE
BUTTERFLY
Endangered

SUMATRAN RHINO
Critically endangered

BORNEAN ORANGUTAN
Critically endangered

AMUR LEOPARD
Critically endangered

BLUE WHALE Endangered

EASTERN LOWLAND GORILLA Critically endangered

HIPPOPOTAMUS Vulnerable

TIGER Endangered

But I DON'T WANT THIS! I don't want there to be fewer animals and plants.

I like there being lots and LOTS of them . . . all different!

I'm glad you said that. There are lots of things we can do to help look after the wonderful web of life.

We need to make sure that creating a habitat for us humans to live in doesn't damage the other living things on Earth. Natural habitats need to be a part of everything we build, so that animals big and small have a place in our cities and towns.

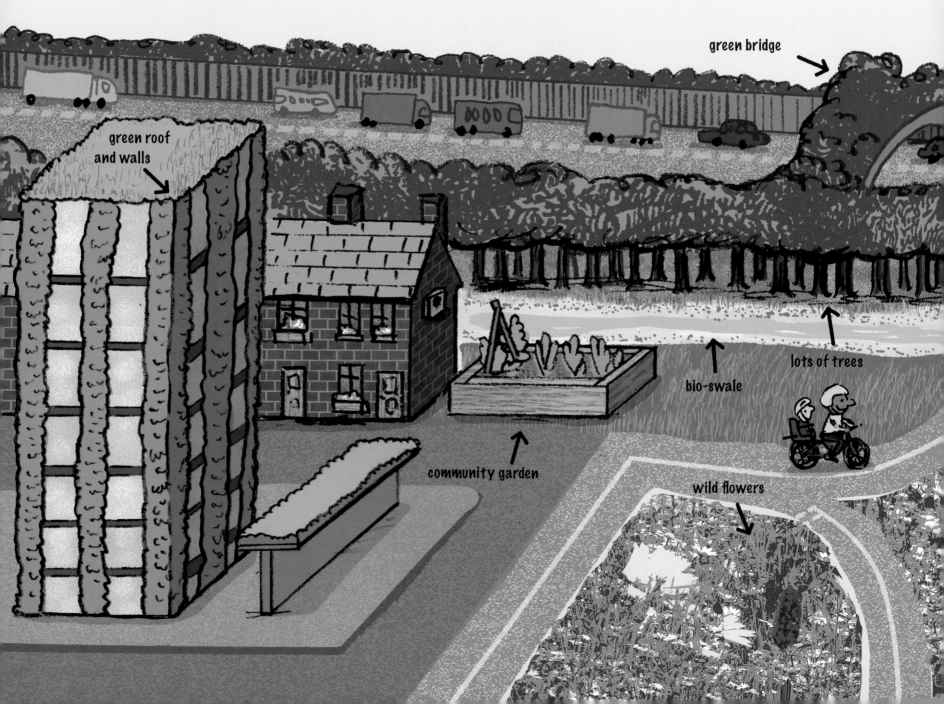

green bridge

green roof and walls

lots of trees

bio-swale

community garden

wild flowers

We need to stop polluting, and make sure our air, water and food are clean.

And the way we make food should change so it doesn't hurt the natural world.
There are better ways to farm, and we don't need to be so greedy when we fish.

The good news is that the natural world is amazing at recovering. When we give it a chance to heal, biodiversity bounces back!

Near the Isle of Arran in Scotland, a no-fishing zone has led to seaweed returning to the sea floor. Lots of baby cod, lobsters and other species now call it home.

NO FISHING

SEEDS SEEDS

At Knepp in Sussex, the owners stopped farming their land and let nature take over. The area is now full of rare creatures and plants not seen for many years.

white storks

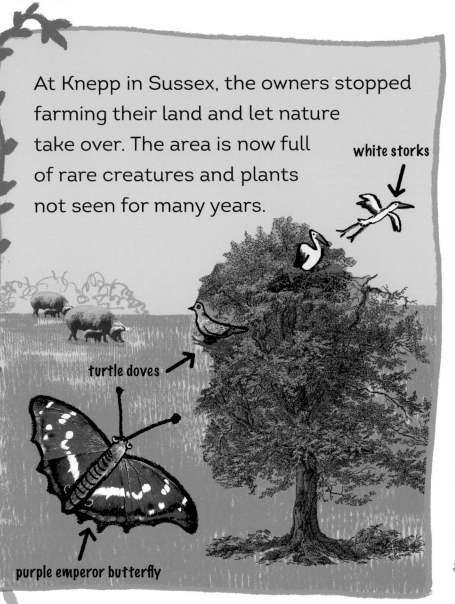

turtle doves

purple emperor butterfly

In Borneo, land corridors are being created so that elephants can move safely between animal reserves.

And in China, a whole forest city is being created that will contain more trees than people.

We are lucky enough to live on a planet brimming with life.

It ALL matters. It's all connected, and we need to remember that we are a part of it.

And if we look after the natural world, we can all live in a happier, healthier world and live happier, healthier lives.

How you can help

There are loads of ways you can support the web of life!

1 Fill a window box with local plants to help insects. Or try to find a small area you can let grow wild, whether it's part of your garden or a verge outside your home.

2 Build or add bug hotels and nest boxes to your garden.

3 Become citizen scientists and observe nature so we can learn how to best protect it.

4 Ask your family to buy organic fruit and vegetables when possible, or even start growing some food yourselves.

LOCAL PRODUCE

5 Make a small pond from a washing-up bowl to create a home for water-loving wildlife.

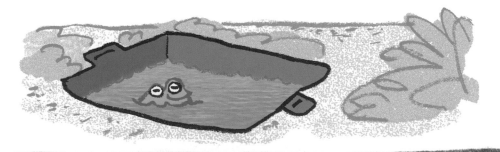

And you know, it's not just grown-ups who have BIG ideas…

DARA MCANULTY is a teenage naturalist in the UK who volunteers with local wildlife groups to record sightings of rare animals, and also helps to rescue bats. In 2018, he raised thousands of pounds so raptor birds in Northern Ireland could be tagged and tracked.

MIKAILA ULMER was only four when she started her company making lemonade sweetened with local honey, but ten years later, her lemonade is sold in 1,500 shops across the USA. Today, 15-year-old Mikaila leads workshops on the importance of honeybees to biodiversity, and donates some of her company's profits to organisations working to save them.

When **JAMMER VEGA** was 17, he invented a fertiliser made from plants near his small village in Peru. This natural product helps local farmers grow cacao (the key ingredient in chocolate), which is becoming more difficult because of climate change.

SO, CAN YOU THINK OF A BIG IDEA TO HELP SAVE THE WEB OF LIFE

?

GLOSSARY

Biodiversity	The incredible variety of plant and animal life in our world.
Bio-swale	A ditch filled with soil and plants that helps prevent flooding after storms.
Green bridge	A bridge across a road or railway line to allow animals to cross safely.
Habitat	The natural home of an animal or plant.
Pollination	When pollen is carried to a flower or plant so it can reproduce.

This book was inspired by David Attenborough, who said:
"No one will protect what they don't care about, and no one will care about what they have never experienced."

Thanks to Dr Sara A Collins, Eco Urban Ranger,
and Andy Ames of Hampshire & Isle of Wight Wildlife Trust.

First published in Great Britain in 2021 by Wren & Rook

HB ISBN: 978 1 5263 6323 7
PB ISBN: 978 1 5263 6321 3
E-book ISBN: 978 1 5263 6322 0
10 9 8 7 6 5 4 3 2 1

MIX
Paper from responsible sources
FSC www.fsc.org
FSC® C104740

Wren & Rook
An imprint of Hachette Children's Group
Part of Hodder & Stoughton
Carmelite House, 50 Victoria Embankment, London EC4Y 0DZ

An Hachette UK Company
www.hachette.co.uk
www.hachettechildrens.co.uk

Managing Editor: Liza Wilde
Art Director: Laura Hambleton
Designer: Alison Still

Printed in China